All Is Mary AND BRIGHT

Piano Solos For Christmas

MARY McDONALD

Editor: Bryan Sharpe
Cover Design: Danielle M. Reinicke

ISBN: 978-0-7877-7318-2

lillenas
PUBLISHING COMPANY

www.lorenz.com

Foreword

The music of Christmas serves as an inviting centerpiece for the holiday season. Shopping centers prepare seasonal displays and lure customers into the festive aisles with familiar songs and carols. Churches fill most December weekends with Hanging of the Greens services, children's choirs, carolers, and meaningful cantatas and musicals all to share the good news of Christ's birth. Spoken to us through scripture, music has breathed life into this gospel story that speaks to the hearts and minds of the receptive listeners, for it is music that brings joy, hope and peace to all believers.

All Is Mary and Bright is an extension of that story offering ten fresh arrangements of carols old and new, carols such as "He Is Born," "The Holly and the Ivy," and classics like "In Dulci Jubilo" and "The Snow Lay On the Ground." One setting is a medley of festive favorites that will make a splendid concert prelude or piano feature in performance. Careful attention has been given to provide a variety of quiet and joyful selections. The tender "Silent Night, Holy Night" is paired with the beautiful "Dona Nobis Pacem" for a Christmas Eve option and one of my personal favorites, "In the Bleak Midwinter." I also included an original "Christmas Lullaby" to share some originality around the beloved "Away In a Manger." There is something for every pianist in this collection, some more challenging than others but all with a charm and expressive, artful touch. Tempo suggestions are offered but feel free to adjust to a comfortable and controllable pace.

Whether for public or private performance, may these songs of the season usher in the warm feelings of Christmas and may our collective offerings be a suitable song for the Savior who came to us on that Holy Night.

—*Mary McDonald*

About the Arranger

Mary McDonald is well known in sacred music. With a career that spans over thirty-five years, her songs appear in the catalogs of every major publisher of church music. More than 800 anthems, seasonal musicals, and keyboard collections testify to her significant contribution to sacred literature.

In 2000, Mary became the first ever woman President of the Southern Baptist Church Music Conference. In addition, she has served as accompanist for the Tennessee Men's Chorale since 1985. Her greatest desire is "to give God glory for the songs He has allowed me to compose. He alone, is the true Creator behind my pen."

In 2011, after serving as sacred music editor for The Lorenz Corporation in Dayton, Ohio for more than twenty years, Mary answered a new call. Now she takes her tremendous passion and love for music making directly to churches as an independent artist. She is in constant demand in churches across the nation for Composer Weekends.

Contents

A Christmas Festival

Arranged by
Mary McDonald
Incorporating familiar carols

*Tune: MENDELSSOHN, Felix Mendelssohn, 1840
Traditional Carol
*This setting was adapted from "Overture" from *Festival of Christmas* (65/2113L)

*Tune: JÜNGST, Hugo Jüngst, ca. 1890
Traditional German Carol

In "2" ♩. = ca. 58

*"Carol of the Bells"**, Mykola Leontovych, 1914
Ukranian Folk Carol

*Tune: **NOËL NOUVELET**, anonymous, 15th Century
Traditional French Carol

Once In Royal David's City

Arranged by **Mary McDonald**
Tune: **IRBY**
by Henry J. Gauntlet (1805-1876)

Duration: 4:00

773182-8

In Dulci Jubilo

Arranged by **Mary McDonald**
Traditional Latin Carol

Joyfully ♩. = c. 86

Duration: 2:20

Do Not
Photocopy

14

He Is Born

Arranged by **Mary McDonald**
Tune: **IL EST NÉ**
Traditional French Carol

Duration: 2:40

Do Not Photocopy

A Christmas Lullaby

Arranged by **Mary McDonald**
Tunes: LUCY by **Johannes Brahms** and
CRADLE SONG by **William J. Kirkpatrick**

Duration: 3:00

773182-21

"Away in a Manger"

The Holly and the Ivy

Arranged by **Mary McDonald**
Traditional French Carol

Duration: 2:30

773182-24

Do Not
Photocopy

The Snow Lay on the Ground

Arranged by **Mary McDonald**
Tune: **VENITE ADOREMUS**
Traditional Carol

Duration: 2:00

773182-28

Bring a Torch, Jeannette, Isabella

Arranged by **Mary McDonald**
Traditional French Carol

Liltingly, not too fast ♩. = c. 62

Duration: 2:30

Do Not
Photocopy

In the Bleak Midwinter

Arranged by **Mary McDonald**
Tune: CRANHAM
Gustav T. Holst (1874-1934)

Duration: 2:50

Do Not
Photocopy

Silent Night, Holy Night

with Dona Nobis Pacem

Arranged by **Mary McDonald**
Tune: **STILLE NACHT**
Franz Gruber

Duration: 3:30

773182-39

Do Not
Photocopy